ENGINEERED BY NATURE

Animal Traps and Lairs

By Louise and
Richard Spilsbury

BELLWETHER MEDIA • MINNEAPOLIS, MN

Jump into the cockpit and
take flight with Pilot books.
Your journey will take you on
high-energy adventures as you
learn about all that is wild,
weird, fascinating, and fun!

This edition first published in 2017 by Bellwether Media, Inc.

No part of this publication may be reproduced in whole or in part without written permission of the publisher.
For information regarding permission, write to Bellwether Media, Inc., Attention: Permissions Department,
5357 Penn Avenue South, Minneapolis, MN 55419.

Library of Congress Cataloging-in-Publication Data

Names: Spilsbury, Louise, author. | Spilsbury, Richard, 1963- author.
Title: Animal Traps and Lairs / by Louise and Richard Spilsbury.
Other titles: Pilot (Bellwether Media)
Description: Minneapolis, MN : Bellwether Media, Inc., 2017. | Series: Pilot.
    Engineered by Nature | Audience: Ages 7-13. | Audience: Grades 3 to
    8. | Includes bibliographical references and index.
Identifiers: LCCN 2016032049 (print) | LCCN 2016036287 (ebook) | ISBN
    9781626175877 (hardcover : alk. paper) | ISBN 9781681033167 (ebook) | ISBN
    9781681033143 delete
Subjects: LCSH: Animal behavior–Juvenile literature. |
    Animals–Habitations–Juvenile literature. | Predatory animals–Juvenile
    literature.
Classification: LCC QL758 .S6494 2017 (print) | LCC QL758 (ebook) | DDC
    591.5-dc23
LC record available at https://lccn.loc.gov/2016032049

Printed in the United States of America, North Mankato, MN.

Table of Contents

Built to Hunt

Animals are **engineered** by nature to survive in their environments. They have **adaptations**, or features, that help them compete with other living things for food.

DID YOU KNOW?

An anglerfish has a long spine that hangs above its mouth. The tip glows in the dark. This light lures prey toward the fish's sharp teeth.

4

FAST FACT

The anglerfish got its name because it has a lure like an angler's fishing pole.

light lure

Animals design and build traps and **lairs** to catch **prey**. Some build physical traps like holes in the ground or sticky webs. Others use trapping behaviors. These **lure** prey toward them, or confuse an animal long enough to grab it. Some animals even use hidden lairs to **ambush** their prey.

Ant Lion Sand Pit

An ant lion **larva** builds its trap in sand. It starts walking backward in a circle. As it walks, it digs. This creates a cone-shaped pit to trap ants.

mandible

DID YOU KNOW?

The larvae of ant lions are known as doodlebugs. This is because the trails they leave behind look like doodles drawn by people.

sand trap

The larva hides at the bottom. Only its **mandibles** rest above the sand. When ants fall in, a well-designed pit guides them toward its mouth.

Some lucky ants survive the fall. As they climb out, the larva throws sand at them. This causes a landslide, carrying the ants back toward the larva's jaws!

FAST FACT

If the pit walls are too steep, sand trickles in. Then the trap collapses. If they are too shallow, ants will not fall in.

Glowworm Larvae Snares

Glowworm larvae often live in dark, damp caves in New Zealand. Without their traps, or snares, they would never eat. From the roof of a cave, they hang lines made from **silk** and beads of sticky **mucus**.

Blue-green light produced by the animals' tails attracts small flying insects. They become trapped in the sticky snares. The lines **vibrate** and alert the larvae of their catch. They then reel in the lines and devour their prey.

FAST FACT

Some larvae hang 70 lines in a single night.

caddisfly

snare

Whale Baleen Trap

Whales are massive. But some feed on the smallest animals in the ocean. **Baleen** whales catch prey by taking in mouthfuls of water. Their giant tongues push the water through baleen plates. These stretch like a stiff curtain from their upper jaws.

A baleen whale has hundreds of plates. They are smooth on the outside. On the inside, they have fringes of bristles. The fringes overlap. This forms a mesh-like strainer. As water passes through, **krill** become trapped. Then the whale swallows!

baleen

FAST FACT

Baleen plates measure from 2 inches (5 centimeters) to 13 feet (4 meters) long.

Engineering in Practice

See baleen in action by creating your own trap. You will need a fine-toothed comb, chopped parsley, and a small tub.

- Fill the tub half full with water.
- Sprinkle in a handful of parsley.
- Use the comb to skim the surface of the water.
- What do you notice? How effective is the "baleen" at capturing food?

Turtle Killer Jaws

An alligator snapping turtle's jaws are a built-in trap. To catch a fish, the turtle finds some murky water. It lies still, waiting, with its jaws wide open. Its eyes scan for prey.

When the turtle's jaws are open, a bright-red piece of flesh is visible in its mouth. Fish are attracted to the flesh. It looks like a juicy worm. When a fish swims in to investigate, the turtle quickly snaps its jaws shut.

DID YOU KNOW?

The alligator snapping turtle stays so still that plants may grow on its back. This makes the turtle almost invisible to fish.

FAST FACT

The turtle swallows small fish whole. It slices larger fish in two with its powerful jaws.

Wild Cat Mimicking

A margay is a wild cat. It catches its prey with a supersmart skill! It searches for a group of tamarin monkeys feeding in the trees. Then it hides nearby.

The cat opens its mouth and lets out a high-pitched squeal. It sounds like the squeal a baby tamarin makes when it is in trouble.

FAST FACT

A margay's flexible ankles can twist 180 degrees.

The tamarins rush to help the "baby." When one climbs down to investigate, the margay leaps out and catches the monkey!

DID YOU KNOW?

Margays have wide, soft feet and flexible toes. This design allows them to hang from branches by just one foot.

tamarin monkey

15

Stoat Hypnosis

Stoats love hunting rabbits. But rabbits are much larger and faster. So, stoats developed an amazing skill. They can **hypnotize** rabbits!

A stoat follows a rabbit for miles. It moves close so the rabbit can see it. Then it starts to act strange. It leaps, flips, twists, and rolls. It ducks in and out of burrow holes.

Slowly, the stoat moves closer. But the rabbit stays put. It cannot take its eyes off the show. Suddenly, the stoat attacks, biting its victim's neck.

FAST FACT

A stoat can take down prey that is 10 times its size.

DID YOU KNOW?

In cold places, stoats change color from brown and white to pure white. This is so they blend in with the snow. Only the tips of their tails stay black.

Humpback Bubble Net

Humpback whales work together to trap fish in a bubble net. One whale dives beneath a **shoal**, making a loud sound. The fish panic and swim upward. Other whales circle around the shoal. This keeps fish from escaping.

The caller swims in an upward spiral, releasing bubbles from its blowhole. The bubbles rise in vertical lines. Together, they form a "net" around the shoal. The fish panic and leap at the surface. The whales then take turns eating.

FAST FACT

A humpback swallows thousands of krill in just one mouthful.

Engineering in Practice

The next time you are in the bath or a swimming pool, try this cool experiment to create a bubble net trap. You will need a small soda bottle with a twisting sports lid.

- Hold the bottle under the water.
- Open the lid a little to release a stream of bubbles.
- Move your hand in a circle to make a ring of bubbles that rise to the surface.
- Now try making an upward spiral shape in the water, like that of a bubble net!

DID YOU KNOW?

The sounds the whales make bounce between the bubbles. This creates a wall of sound. Fish avoid the wall because it makes their bodies vibrate and feel uncomfortable.

Praying Mantis Disguise

A praying mantis uses disguise to trap prey. As it moves, it gently rocks. It looks like a green leaf swaying in the breeze.

To hunt, the mantis raises its long front legs. It stays still until an insect passes by. Suddenly, it lunges its neck forward, stretching out its legs.

FAST FACT

The praying mantis is named for the way it sits while waiting for prey.

Sharp spikes on the mantis's legs trap the insect. The attack is lightning fast. With its victim captured, the mantis slowly devours it alive.

Moray Eel Hole

Moray eels can make a lair almost anywhere. Even a hole in a shipwreck can be an eel hideout. Their skin is coated with mucus so they can easily slip into their lairs. There, they lie in wait.

A moray attacks by biting with its large jaws. Then a second set of jaws slides forward. These sharp teeth grip the victim. They also pull the prey toward the moray's stomach. At the same time, the outer jaws chomp away.

DID YOU KNOW?

A moray sometimes comes out of its lair to attack larger prey. It winds its snakelike body around its victim. This holds prey still while the moray feeds.

Morays have poor
eyesight. They
use their sense
of smell to hunt.

Shrimp Stun Trap

A mantis shrimp hides in a small crack in a **coral reef**. Its tough, club-like claws are folded under its head. The claws have spikes that **impale** victims. When prey comes near, the shrimp is ready to strike.

DID YOU KNOW?

The mantis shrimp has large eyes that stand out on stalks. They give the shrimp incredibly good eyesight. It is able to spot prey that is difficult to see.

claws

The shrimp's blows are fast and strong. The victim does not know what hit it. This powerful claw swipe also creates a bubble of air. When the bubble bursts, it sends **shock waves** through the water that **stun** prey.

Spider Trapdoor

To build a hidden lair, the trap-door spider digs a hole in the ground. It lines this hole with sand, **saliva**, and silk. It uses these materials to make a D-shaped trapdoor over the hole.

The spider waits inside. It feels the vibrations of a passing victim through the silk threads. Suddenly, it throws open the trapdoor. The spider grabs the prey in its powerful jaws. **Venom** keeps the prey still. Then the spider drags its victim inside and feasts.

DID YOU KNOW?

In some trapdoors, you can see rings. These show how the trap has grown each year, as the spider has grown bigger. They are a little like the rings in a tree trunk!

trapdoor

ACTIVITY
Engineering in Practice

The trapdoor works because the spider
makes silk hinges. A hinge is a type of
machine called a lever. A push from
the spider on the inside of the trapdoor
turns it around a fixed point. This is
called a pivot. Try this experiment to
find out how trapdoors work.

- Try to push open a door from the
  side away from the hinges. Then
  try pushing from the side close
  to the hinges.
- Which side requires the bigger push?
  Can you figure out why?

Engineered to Survive

Chasing prey uses a lot of energy. Animals that use traps and lairs can wait for prey to come to them. They only use energy when they have to.

DID YOU KNOW?

Leopard seals are fast swimmers. But they save energy by hanging out in the water under icy ledges. There, they wait for penguins to jump in.

Some animals hunt for food and also use traps or lairs. Others rely entirely on traps and lairs to survive. Some live in places where many animals feed on similar prey. Others live where there is little food. These animals are engineered by nature to be good hunters.

FAST FACT

A leopard seal can devour a penguin in less than seven minutes.

Glossary

adaptations—features or characteristics that an organism has that help it survive

ambush—to attack by surprise

baleen—strands of tough material that hang down from the upper jaw of some whales; also describes the kinds of whales with this feature.

coral reef—a structure made of coral that usually grows in shallow seawater

engineered—designed and built

hypnotize—to put something in a sleeplike state

impale—to stab through

krill—very small, shrimplike ocean animals

lairs—places where animals rest that are often hidden

larva—the immature form of an insect

lure—to draw in; something that attracts something to something else.

mandibles—sharp jaws

mucus—a slimy substance

prey—animals that are eaten by other animals

saliva—spit

shoal—a large group of fish swimming together

shock waves—waves formed by a sharp change in pressure

silk—fine threads made by spiders and some insects

stun—to confuse an animal's senses, usually by a blow

venom—poison produced by some animals

vibrate—to move continuously and quickly back and forth

To Learn More

AT THE LIBRARY

Buckley, Jim. *Spiders and Other Deadly Animals*. New York, N.Y.: DK Children, 2016.

Kovacs, Vic. *Spiders and Other Animals That Make Traps*. New York, N.Y.: Windmill Books, 2015.

Wilson, Emily. *Trap-Door Spiders*. New York, N.Y.: PowerKids Press, 2016.

ON THE WEB

Learning more about animal traps and lairs is as easy as 1, 2, 3.

1. Go to www.factsurfer.com.
2. Enter "animal traps and lairs" into the search box.
3. Click the "Surf" button and you will see a list of related websites.

With factsurfer.com, finding more information is just a click away.

The images in this book are reproduced through the courtesy of: Fenkieandreas/ Shutterstock, front cover, pp. 1, 22–23; Helmut Corneli/ Getty Images, pp. 4–5; VaughanJessnitz/ Shutterstock, pp. 6–7; iHereArt/ Shutterstock, p. 7 (top); Markus Thomenius/ Alamy Stock Photo, pp. 8–9; Bruce Marlin/ Wikipedia, p. 9 (top right); John Tunney/ Shutterstock, pp. 10–11; Ryan M. Bolton/ Shutterstock, pp. 12–13; Tom Brakefield/ Getty Images, pp. 14–15; Nattanan726/ Shutterstock, p. 15 (right); Bildagentur Zoonar GmbH/ Shutterstock, pp. 16–17; Mitsuaki Iwago/ Minden Pictures/ Getty Images, pp. 18–19; Alex Sun/ Shutterstock, pp. 20–21; Magnusdeepbelow/ Shutterstock, pp. 24–25; Marshal Hedin/ Flickr, pp. 26–27; Ben Cranke/ Nature Picture Library, pp. 28–29.